THE VIRGIN MARY MOTHER OF GOD

BLESSED ABOVE ALL WOMEN

AUTHOR ILLUSTRATOR - MARIA ATHANASIOU

Bibliography:

Orthodox Study Bible, Holy Tradition, Great Friday Evening Lamentations by Patmos Press, The Life of the Virgin Mary the Theotokos by Holy Apostles Convent, The Gospel of James, The Synaxarion.

To order additional copies of this book, contact:
Xlibris
844-714-8691
www.Xlibris.com
Orders@Xlibris.com

ISBN:	Softcover	978-1-4535-7747-9
	Hardcover	978-1-4535-7748-6
	EBook	978-1-4771-6734-2

Print information available on the last page

Rev. date: 05/15/2024

DEDICATION

AXION ESTI

"It is truly worthy to bless Thee,

O Theotokos, ever blessed and

Most pure, and the Mother of our God"

JERUSALEM BEFORE THE SAVIOR

According to the ancient tradition of the Church, Jerusalem in Judea was suffering under the Roman Empire before the birth of Jesus. Everyone was anxiously waiting for the Savior, the promised Messiah the prophets had prophesied about, who was to come and save the world.

Messiah is the mediator between God and the world.

PRAYING FAITHFULLY

Joachim was a rich man from Nazareth of Galilee, a descendant of the royal family of David from the tribe of Judah. He was a shepherd, owner of many sheep. He loved and feared God and offered part of his wealth to the Temple of God and part to support the needy, for the forgiveness of his sins and the salvation of his soul. He married Anna, one of the three daughters of the priest Matthan from the tribe of Levi. Joachim and Anna were married for many years and had reached an old age but they had no children because Anna was barren. They were both praying faithfully to God for a child, promising to dedicate it back to Him.

Barren is childless. To be a barren woman then was considered shameful.

THE GOOD NEWS

Joachim went up on a mountain with his sheep to fast and pray to God, asking for the blessing of a child. After forty days of ascetic life, an angel appeared to him and said, "I am Gabriel who presents your prayers and your alms to God and He has heard your prayers! You will have a daughter, and you shall name her Mary. She will be **blessed above all women** and shall bring forth the Savior of the world." Then the same angel that gave the good news to Joachim on the mountain appeared to Anna also, while she was walking in her garden and gave her the good news.

Gabriel is the Archangel of the Annunciation, a messenger of God.

THE GOLDEN GATE

The angel also told Anna to run to the Golden Gate of the Temple to meet there Joachim who was coming back home.

Joachim and Anna are the Holy & Righteous Ancestors of God.

THE BIRTH OF THE THEOTOKOS

Nine months later Anna gave birth to a daughter, as the angel said and they called her Mary. God reserved for Joachim and Anna this special blessing that brought great joy, happiness and salvation to the whole world. The great feast of the birth of Mary, the Panagia, the Mother of God, is celebrated on September 8th, and both heaven and earth rejoice.

Theotokos is the Mother of God. She gave birth to Jesus Christ our God and Savior who granted us eternal life.
Panagia is All Holy.

MARY IN THE TEMPLE

Joachim and Anna kept their promise to God and when Mary was three they brought her to the Temple in Jerusalem, to the service of God, as a thanksgiving gift. The prophet Zacharias, the husband of Elizabeth, who was the high priest of the Temple, enlightened by the Holy Spirit, brought Mary to the Holy of Holies. Zacharias recognized Mary to be the virgin of Isaiah's Prophesy.

The Holy of Holies was the most sacred place in the Temple. It was sacred with the presence of God and only the high priest was allowed there once a year.

Therefore the Lord Himself will give you a sign: behold, the virgin shall conceive, and bear a Son, and you shall call His name Immanuel.
Isaiah 7:14

FOOD FROM HEAVEN

According to the Gospel of Saint James, Mary grew up in the Holy of Holies. Every day angels came down from heaven and brought her food from God to purify her and prepare her to receive Jesus Christ our Lord. The food the angels brought to Mary became Christ for us; the bread from heaven.

Mary was happy to be near God. She was blessed with wisdom. She studied and learned the Holy Scriptures. She prayed, fasted and amazed the angels with the beauty of her soul. Mary's parents Joachim and Anna came to the Temple often to visit her until they fell asleep to the Lord.

JOSEPH THE HUSBAND OF MARY

When Mary became a teenager, she could no longer stay in the Temple according to the Jewish custom. While Zacharias was praying to God asking who Mary's guardian should be, he saw an angel who told him to call all the local widowers with their rods and God would show him with a sign who the guardian of Mary should be. Zacharias did as the angel told him. The sign from God appeared as a flower on the rod of Joseph, the elderly carpenter from Nazareth who was a descendant of the family of King David. He accepted to be betrothed to Mary and be her fatherly guardian because this was the will of God, and Mary left the Temple of Jerusalem and followed Joseph in Galilee.

There shall come forth a rod from the root of **Jesse**, and a flower shall grow out of his root. The Spirit of God shall rest upon Him, the Spirit of wisdom and understanding, the Spirit of counsel and might, the Spirit of knowledge and godliness. **Isaiah 11:1-2**

Jesse was the father of King David.
The rod represents the Virgin Mary and **the blossom** Jesus Christ.
Betrothed is engaged to be married. At that time when betrothed, the bride lived in the husband's house who was her guardian and provider.

THE ANNUNCIATION

One day when Mary was outside getting water at the well, she heard a voice in the wind but because she did not see anyone, she ran inside and sat to weave with the purple thread. Then she saw the angel.

And having come in, the angel said to her, "Rejoice, highly favored one, the Lord is with you; **blessed are you among women!**" But when she saw him, she was troubled at his saying, and considered what manner of greeting this was. Then the angel said to her, "Do not be afraid, Mary, for you have found favor with God. And behold, you will conceive in your womb and bring forth a Son, and shall call His name JESUS. He will be great, and will be called the Son of the Highest; and the Lord God will give Him the throne of His father David. And He will reign over the house of Jacob forever, and of His kingdom there will be no end."

Then Mary said to the angel, "How can this be, since I do not know a man?" And the angel answered and said to her, "The Holy Spirit will come upon you, and the power of the Highest will overshadow you; therefore, also, that Holy One who is to be born will be called the Son of God. Now indeed, Elizabeth your relative has also conceived a son in her old age; and this is now the sixth month for her who was called barren. For with God nothing will be impossible." Then Mary said, "Behold the maidservant of the **Lord!** Let it be to me according to your word." And the angel departed from her. **Luke 1:28-38**

THE VISIT TO ELIZABETH

Now Mary arose in those days and went into the hill country with haste, to a city of Judah, and entered the house of Zacharias and greeted Elizabeth. And it happened, when Elizabeth heard the greeting of Mary, that the babe leaped in her womb; and Elizabeth was filled with the Holy Spirit. Then she spoke out with a loud voice and said, "**Blessed are you among women**, and blessed is the fruit of your womb! But why is this granted to me, that the mother of my Lord should come to me? For indeed, as soon as the voice of your greeting sounded in my ears, the babe leaped in my womb for joy. Blessed is she who believed, for there will be a fulfillment of those things which were told her from the Lord."

And Mary said: "My soul magnifies the Lord, and my spirit has rejoiced in God my Savior. For He has regarded the lowly state of His maidservant; **for behold, henceforth all generations will call me blessed." Luke 1:39-48**

Good things and the grace of God come to those who make Jesus Lord in their lives. The grace of God is recognized by others as Elizabeth recognized the grace when she saw Mary.

JOSEPH'S DREAM

When Joseph saw Mary expecting a child, his heart was broken, and was troubled about how this had happened, and who had deceived Mary who grew up in the Holy of Holies eating heavenly bread from the hand of an angel.

Then Joseph her husband, being a just man, and not wanting to make her a public example, was minded to put her away secretly. But while he thought about these things, behold, an angel of the Lord appeared to him in a dream, saying, "Joseph, son of David, do not be afraid to take to you Mary your wife, for that which is conceived in her is of the Holy Spirit. And she will bring forth a Son, and you shall call His name JESUS, for He will save His people from their sins."

So all this was done that it might be fulfilled which was spoken by the Lord through the prophet, saying: "Behold, the virgin shall be with child, and bear a Son, and they shall call His name Immanuel," which is translated, "God with us." **Matthew 1:19-23**

THE NATIVITY OF JESUS CHRIST

And it came to pass in those days that a decree went out from Caesar Augustus that all the world should be registered. This census first took place while Quirinius was governing Syria. So all went to be registered, everyone to his own city. Joseph also went up from Galilee, out of the city of Nazareth, into Judea, to the city of David, which is called **Bethlehem**, because he was of the house and lineage of David, to be registered with Mary, his betrothed wife, who was with child. So it was, that while they were there, the days were completed for her to be delivered. And she brought forth her firstborn Son, and wrapped Him in swaddling cloths, and laid Him in a manger, because there was no room for them in the inn. **Luke 2:1-7**

Bethlehem means the "House of Bread". Jesus Himself said: "I am the living bread which came down from heaven. If anyone eats of this bread, he will live forever; and the bread that I shall give is My flesh, which I shall give for the life of the world." **John 6:51**

When we receive the Holy Communion we receive that saving bread from heaven.

THE WISE MEN FROM THE EAST

Now after Jesus was born in Bethlehem of Judea in the days of Herod the king, behold, wise men from the East came to Jerusalem, saying, "Where is He who has been born King of the Jews? For we have seen His star in the East and have come to worship Him." When Herod the king heard this, he was troubled, and all Jerusalem with him. And when he had gathered all the chief priests and scribes of the people together, he inquired of them where the Christ was to be born. So they said to him, "In Bethlehem of Judea, for thus it is written by the prophet: **Matthew 2:1-5**

The Magi came to Bethlehem following the big star in the sky and when they saw the Child with His Mother Mary, they fell on their knees and worshipped Him and offered Him gifts of gold, frankincense and myrrh. Then, warned by an angel, that Herod is seeking to kill the Child, they returned home from a different way.

The Magi were wise men, astrologers and kings from the Far East seeking the Lord. They traveled to Bethlehem, where they found the New Born King.

THE PRESENTATION OF THE LORD

Joseph and Mary brought Jesus to the Temple 40 days after His birth, with an offering of two pigeons. The Righteous Simeon, who was waiting for the Messiah and was promised by God that he would not die before he saw Christ, met them at the Temple and inspired by the Holy Spirit, recognized the Child to be the Savior and said: "Lord, now You are letting Your servant depart in peace, according to Your word; for my eyes have seen Your salvation which You have prepared before the face of all peoples, a light to bring revelation to the Gentiles, and the glory of Your people Israel." And Joseph and His mother marveled at those things which were spoken of Him. Then Simeon blessed them, and said to Mary His mother, "Behold, this Child is destined for the fall and rising of many in Israel, and for a sign which will be spoken against (yes, a sword will pierce through your own soul also), that the thoughts of many hearts may be revealed." **Luke 2:29-35**

As Jesus was brought to the Temple when He was 40 days old, so Christian parents bring their babies to Church when they are 40 days old also.

THE FLIGHT TO EGYPT

Now when they had departed, behold, an angel of the Lord appeared to Joseph in a dream, saying, "Arise, take the young Child and His mother, flee to Egypt, and stay there until I bring you word; for Herod will seek the young Child to destroy Him." When he arose, he took the young Child and His mother by night and departed for Egypt, and was there until the death of Herod that it might be fulfilled which was spoken by the Lord through the prophet, saying, *"Out of Egypt I called My Son."* **Matthew 2:13-15**

The trip to Egypt from Bethlehem on a donkey was a long and dangerous one. The Holy Family traveled for several weeks and passed the desert and many villages and towns. All the places they passed were blessed by their presence. They stayed in Egypt for three years, to protect the life of Jesus, until the angel appeared to Joseph again.

THE RETURN TO NAZARETH

Now when Herod was dead, behold, an angel of the Lord appeared in a dream to Joseph in Egypt, saying, "Arise, take the young Child and His mother, and go to the land of Israel, for those who sought the young Child's life are dead." Then he arose, took the young Child and His mother, and came into the land of Israel. But when he heard that Archelaus was reigning over Judea instead of his father Herod, he was afraid to go there. And being warned by God in a dream, he turned aside into the region of Galilee. And he came and dwelt in a city called Nazareth that it might be fulfilled which was spoken by the prophets, "He shall be called a Nazarene." **Matthew 2:19-23**

JESUS IN THE TEMPLE

Jesus taught the Word of God for the first time at the Passover when he was twelve and went with His Holy Mother and Joseph on a pilgrimage to Jerusalem from Nazareth. He entered the Temple, sat in the middle of the teachers and amazed them with His wisdom and His knowledge of the Holy Scriptures.

When the feast of the Passover ended Jesus did not follow the pilgrims back to Nazareth. Joseph and Mary realized that Jesus was not among their relatives on the way back to Nazareth and being greatly troubled they returned to Jerusalem to look for Him. They found Him in the Temple after three days.

And He said to them, "Why did you seek Me? Did you not know that I must be about My Father's business?" But they did not understand the statement which He spoke to them. Then He went down with them and came to Nazareth, and was subject to them, but His mother kept all these things in her heart. And Jesus increased in wisdom and stature, and in favor with God and men. **Luke 2:49-52**

THE CARPENTER, THE SON OF MARY

Joseph, the devoted guardian of the Holy family, was the village carpenter, and Jesus grew up next to him and worked as a carpenter also. Joseph had seven children from his first wife Salome, three daughters and four sons called the brothers of the Lord. When Jesus was thirty years old He started His ministry and called His twelve disciples.

And when the Sabbath had come, He began to teach in the synagogue. And many hearing Him were astonished, saying, "Where did this Man get these things? And what wisdom is this which is given to Him, that such mighty works are performed by His hands! Is this not the carpenter, the Son of Mary, and brother of James, Joses, Judas, and Simon? And are not His sisters here with us?" So they were offended at Him. **Mark 6:2-3**

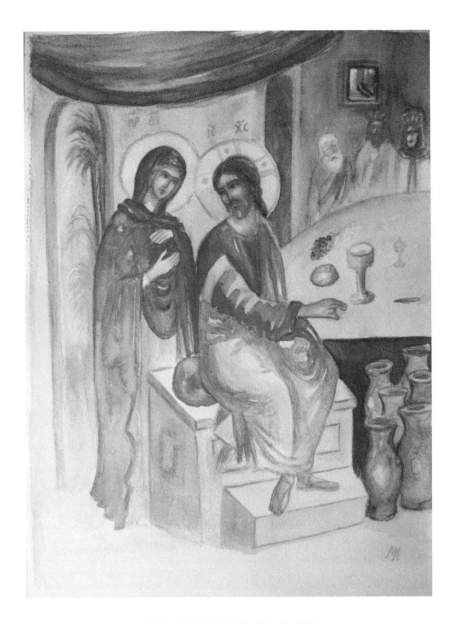

THE WEDDING IN CANA

Now both Jesus and His disciples were invited to the wedding. And when they ran out of wine, the mother of Jesus said to Him, "They have no wine." Jesus said to her, "Woman, what does your concern have to do with Me? My hour has not yet come." His mother said to the servants, "Whatever He says to you, do it." **John 2:2-5**

Even though it was not time for Jesus to start His miracles, He honored His Mother's request and blessed the water turning it into fine wine. This was the first miracle of Jesus and many at the wedding believed in Him.

The Gospel of this first miracle is read at the wedding sacrament as a reminder that a marriage at the Church, the house of God, is blessed and will succeed with His Blessings. His Holy Mother is always interceding on our behalf to Jesus when we pray and ask for Her help and she reminds us today "whatever He says to you do it".

THE PASSOVER

The Virgin Mary followed Her Son and witnessed His amazing miracles, His love and compassion. She saw Him heal the sick, raise the dead, feed the multitudes and teach the Gospel. She always remembered the words of Simeon "a sword will pierce through your own soul" but kept all these worries in her heart, until three years later when it was time again to go to Jerusalem for the Passover.

Now Jesus, going up to Jerusalem, took the twelve disciples aside on the road and said to them, "Behold, we are going up to Jerusalem, and the Son of Man will be betrayed to the chief priests and to the scribes; and they will condemn Him to death, and deliver Him to the Gentiles to mock and to scourge and to crucify. And the third day He will rise again."
Matthew 20:17-19

EXTREME HUMILITY

It all happened as He told them. The Mother of God cried for her Sweet Jesus.

O my sweet springtime, my sweetest Child,
to where has Your beauty vanished?

THE CROSS

Now there stood by the cross of Jesus His mother, and His mother's sister, Mary the wife of Clopas, and Mary Magdalene. When Jesus therefore saw His mother, and the disciple whom He loved standing by, He said to His mother, "Woman, behold your son!" Then He said to the disciple, "Behold your mother!" And from that hour that disciple took her to his own home. **John 19:25-27**

The Cross was the sword in Mary's heart. It is the symbol of salvation. Even when Jesus Christ was on the Cross, at the worst moments of His earthly life, He still cared for us, as it is indicated by offering Panagia, His All Holy Mother, to the protection of His disciple John and vice versa.

JESUS BURIED IN JOSEPH'S TOMB

Now behold, there was a man named Joseph, a council member, a good and just man. He had not consented to their decision and deed. He was from Arimathea, a city of the Jews, who himself was also waiting for the kingdom of God. This man went to Pilate and asked for the body of Jesus. Then he took it down, wrapped it in linen, and laid it in a tomb that was hewn out of the rock, where no one had ever lain before.

Luke 23:50-53

THE RESURRECTION

Three days later, early on Sunday morning, when the Virgin Mary and Mary Magdalene went to the tomb of Jesus with myrrh, they found it empty. An angel, dressed in dazzling white, was sitting on the stone of the tomb and told them that Jesus is risen!

And as they went to tell His disciples, behold, Jesus met them, saying, "Rejoice!" So they came and held Him by the feet and worshiped Him. Then Jesus said to them, "Do not be afraid. Go and tell My brethren to go to Galilee, and there they will see Me." **Matthew 28:9-10**

THE ASCENSION

Jesus was appearing to His Apostles for 40 days. He told them to wait in Jerusalem for the Holy Spirit. Then on the fortieth day when the Virgin Mary and the Apostles were with Him up on the Mount of Olives, He ascended into heaven in the clouds.

And while they looked steadfastly toward heaven as He went up, behold, two men stood by them in white apparel, who also said, "Men of Galilee, why do you stand gazing up into heaven? This same Jesus, who was taken up from you into heaven, will so come in like manner as you saw Him go into heaven."
Acts 1:10-11

THE PENTECOST

The Mother of God and the Apostles were all in the Upper Room in Jerusalem praying and waiting for the promise of God, the Holy Spirit.

When the Day of Pentecost had fully come, they were all with one accord in one place. And suddenly there came a sound from heaven, as of a rushing mighty wind, and it filled the whole house where they were sitting. Then there appeared to them divided **tongues, as of fire,** and one sat upon each of them. And they were all filled with the Holy Spirit and began to speak with other tongues, as the Spirit gave them utterance. **Acts 2:1-4**

The Pentecost is the day the Holy Spirit came, as tongues of fire, fifty days after the Resurrection of Jesus Christ and the Apostles started to teach the Word of God.
The Holy Spirit is the Comforter that comes when we pray.

THE FIRST ICON OF THE PANAGIA

The Evangelist Luke from Antioch, the writer of the second Gospel and the Acts was one of the 70 and a fellow worker of Paul. He also was a physician and a painter. Legend has it that he was the first artist to paint the first portrait of the Virgin Mary. He showed his love by putting together Her Holy image and Her kindness, as he saw Her and through this icon we know Her look.

Saint Luke painted other icons also and so he started the sacred art of iconography. The Holy Mother saw the finished icons, approved of them and blessed them. She prayed that the grace of Jesus would be on them. Icons are the Gospel in color with pictures, windows to Heaven. The feast day of Saint Luke is October 18.

THE HOLY SEPULCHRE

The All Holy Theotokos lived in Jerusalem, in the house of John. She loved to visit Bethlehem, the Mount of Olives, the Holy Sepulchre and all the Holy Places where Jesus walked on earth that brought back sweet memories of Him. There she kneeled, burnt incense and prayed to Her Son and God. Many Christians came to Jerusalem to see the Mother of God and receive her blessings, and they followed her to these Sacred Places to pray with Her to Jesus. This is how the pilgrimages to the Holy Land started.

In the center of the old city of Jerusalem, on the hill of Golgotha, over the Sacred Tomb of Jesus is built the Church of the Holy Sepulchre. There at the site of the Crucifixion, the Burial and the Resurrection of Christ a great miracle happens at Easter every year in front of thousands of witnesses. The Holy Light flashes from the depth of the Sepulchre in a supernatural way.

THE DORMITION OF PANAGIA

Tradition has it that the Archangel Gabriel appeared to the Theotokos one day when she was on the Mount of Olives praying, and foretold her that in three days she will depart for Paradise, and gave her a shiny palm branch from heaven.

The Apostles at that time were in far away places teaching the Gospel of Jesus. They were brought supernaturally to Jerusalem to John's house, caught miraculously in angelic clouds by the will of God to be with Panagia, all except Thomas.

It was August 15 Sunday morning. The Apostles were gathered around the Virgin Mary singing hymns and praying, when suddenly a bright lightening filled the room and Jesus appeared in all His glory, with all His angels and took into His arms the pure soul of His Holy Mother, wrapped up like a newborn baby in swaddling clothes, to transport it to Heaven.
The Apostles laid the body of the All Holy Mother to rest in a tomb in Gethsemane and covered the entrance with a large stone.

Dormition is falling asleep to the Lord. The Dormition of the Panagia is celebrated on August 15.

THE TRANSLATION OF THE THEOTOKOS

When Thomas arrived three days later, according to the tradition of the Holy Orthodox Church, all the Apostles together went to the tomb of Panagia but they found it empty. Her body was not there. They prayed to God asking where the Body of the Mother of God is. That evening the All Holy Mother appeared to the disciples in the sky, surrounded by angels and said to them, "Rejoice I will be with you always".

The Virgin Mary, Mother of God and Mother to all the brothers and sisters of Jesus is invisibly protecting and guiding those who pray to Her, asking for Her intercessions to God Her Son.

Translation is change from temporary to eternal state.

THE HOLY LAND

This is the entrance to the Tomb of the Virgin Mary at the base of the Mount of Olives in Jerusalem, the Holy Land.

MOUNT ATHOS GREECE

The Great Lavra is the first monastery that was built on Mount Athos in the 10th century. According to the legend, Saint Athanasios the Athonite, who was building the monastery, had a vision of the Virgin Mary when he ran out of money and food to continue. The Virgin Mary appeared to him and told him that he would have everything he would need, in abundance and she told him to strike the earth with his rod. Then a miracle happened. A stream of water began to flow out of the rocks. That spring is still flowing with healing water, today.

Since then many monasteries were built on the Holy Mountain also known as the Garden of the Virgin Mary. In honor of the Panagia no women are allowed there. It is populated by Monks from around the world who dedicated their lives to praise God and keep His commandments. In the Monasteries and the Churches of the Holy Mountain survive many miracle working icons of the Virgin Mary.

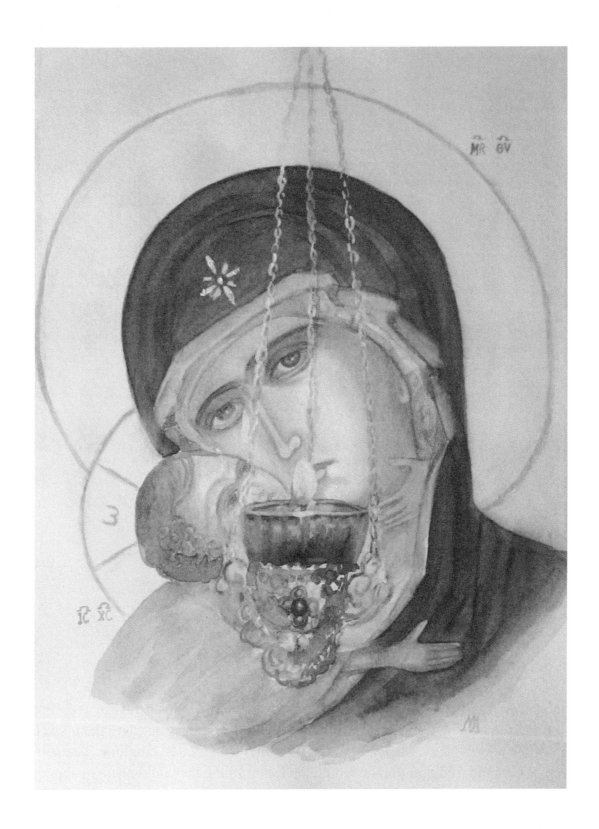

THE ANGELIC SALUTATION

Hail! Mary, Keharitomeni "full of grace", the Lord is with thee. O Virgin Theotokos, blessed art thou among women, and blessed is the fruit of thy womb, for thou hast borne the Savior of our souls.